Is He Worth It?

Is He Worth It?

Based on a True Story

Latasha Freeman

Copyright © 2008 by Latasha Freeman.

Library of Congress Control Number: 2008902263
ISBN: Hardcover   978-1-4363-2818-0
               Softcover   978-1-4363-2817-3

All rights reserved. No part of this book may be reproduced or transmitted in any form or by any means, electronic or mechanical, including photocopying, recording, or by any information storage and retrieval system, without permission in writing from the copyright owner.

Print information available on the last page.

Rev. date: 10/10/2018

To order additional copies of this book, contact:
Xlibris
1-888-795-4274
www.Xlibris.com
Orders@Xlibris.com
561882

CONTENTS

People I Want to Thank 7

A Lesson to Learn 9

Part 1: The Beginning 15

Part 2: What in the Hell Was I Thinking? 27

Part 3: The Rough Move 33

Part 4: Drama 37

Part 5: The Good Times 43

Part 6: A New Love 49

Part 7: Ms. Thang 55

Part 8: The Stalking Begins 61

Part 9: Enough Is Enough 69

Part 10: Joining the Military 75

Part 11: FBI Is Looking for Me 81

Part 12: Back to "T" Town 87

People I Want to Thank

First and foremost, *God*! He is the head of my life. I love him so much for making this happen and for keeping me safe and in his arms.

Family, friends, and my mom for teaching me and telling me to never depend on a man for nothing. Always be independent, make your own money, and take care of home first. For being my best friend and my mother. For always loving me and helping me when you could. I Love You Ma.

My daddy, for always being there for me, always being my friend, and letting me know when I'm wrong. For being the peacemaker when things got crazy in the house. For teaching me to always put God first in everything I do, and for reminding me that God is a jealous God and that if you treasure something, he will take it away. I Love You Daddy.

My children—Cassandra, Shantell, Charda, and Charles Jr. They are the love of my life. My children helped me through so many rough times. They wiped my tears away when I was crying, they made me laugh when I was hurting, and they always used to tell me, "Ma, don't worry, it will be okay." Thank you, my babies. I love y'all so much.

I want to thank my friends Robert Cook, Sharon A. Campbell, Lorenzo McElveen and Willie & Peggy Daniels for being a inspiration in my life. My sister Karen Hills for being my number one fan and always believing in me. For being my riding partner and always having sis back. My brothers Pookie, Donnell and Kelvin for teaching me the street life and for there love and support in everything I do. I would also like to think Kevin Bellamy for giving his shoulder to cry on when I was hurting and for always being my friend. I love you!

I want to thank my auntie Mary for all her support when I was deployed, for all the uplifting e-mails and mail. My auntie Addie J. for being there for me when I was in trouble and no one else was there. I would like to say Hi to my oldest sister Tonyanita. I love you all.

A Lesson to Learn

Here I sit in confusion, wondering were did I go wrong and why the man I loved for many years is now gone.

I gave you love, compassion, and friendship—all that I had. I gave you all of my time, even in my dreams; yet I wake up lonely, yearning for your touch. All I feel is emptiness. I miss you so much.

What is it that she has and I don't? Love, sex, friendship, power, or all of the above. I gave you four beautiful children, she gave you none. I gave you a lifetime commitment. Wasn't that enough? The lies for no reason, the cheating throughout the season. Yet I'm still yearning for your love.

See, faithful she could never be. She's not a woman, she's a girl. A real woman can get her own man, not someone else's man—and that you fail to realize, through the darkness of her sneaky eyes.

The time will come when she leaves you high and dry for another man. Don't come back to me for another chance. I gave you my heart, the one you've broken; foolish of me to believe you could be faithful and never cheat. I thought you were the one, but now I see.

You will be back crying and begging on your knees. "Think about the kids," you will say. FUCK YOU! You coward, no how, no way.

A lesson you will learn, indeed you will—never leave a good thing for a cheap thrill.

Let me give you a little background about me. Well, I'm not your typical woman. I'm very much an independent, caring, trustworthy, loving-you lady. And when I fall in love, I fall hard—which is my downfall, but I'm working on that. I work a nine-to-five, and I am also self-employed at night. I've had my share of fun and tears; but through it all, I've learned along the way, and I've become closer to my kids and God. I wouldn't change that for the world. I have some go-getters for kids, and I love it. I tell them all the time they should have been boys. I mean, I've done some things in my life, but my girls take it to a whole other level. Fight! It's like a hobby for them, I had to slow them down. I can't blame them, because they get it from there mother, because I was the same way. Sometimes, I think God is bringing my past back to kick me in my face. I mean, when you think you have gotten away with something somehow, you do see it again. In my case, I see it through my girls. Then again, it's not too bad, they're not planning to rob anyone. You know, like, one day you and your boys are sitting around broke as hell, working, and every little extra change you have has to go on a bill that seems to be extra high that month when normally it's a lot lower. Ya'll are not playing to go to an apartment complex for college students, wait for one of them to leave, because one of your boys has already scoped the place out. Wait until they leave, then you and two of your boys go in while the other partner is waiting in the car. You and your boys are in and out in about five minutes, and ya'll are running down the street to the car with a TV, radio, DVD, clothes, and other small items. Ya'll are running to the car and getting to the car only for the driver to drive the FUCK OFF! I mean your hand is on the handle, and this scary asshole drives off. Now you and your boys are running after the car, telling the dumbass to stop. He finally stops, then everyone gets in, and the one with the TV slaps the shit out of the driver. Then the driver pulls off, crying like a bitch; he pulls out in front of a bus, and then you see your life flash before your eyes. Then all anyone in the car can do is holler. But you make it, and then the driver gets it together and drives on. I guess he was thinking about that last slap. I can say they are not doing anything like that, or you and your girls are in high school and decided to skip school and go to the projects (of course) to go see what is happening; and a guy friend wants a ride to the mall, so you give him a ride, and he doesn't want to put in on the gas, but flashes a pocketful of money. Driver tells him how she feels, and he wants to talk shit to the driver. Now mind you, he is getting a ride, so how in the hell are you going to talk shit to someone when you are in their shit? Hello! How smart can you be? So the driver tells her girls to take his money then push his ass out the car. The boy gets drunk and says no one is going to touch him. Now mind you, the driver is a thug and acts just like a boy, but loves dick all day. Her girls take some of his money, but the driver sees that they left a little knot, so she tells the passenger to grab the wheel, and reaches back, takes all his money, tells her partner to open the door, then pushes the boy out of the car, onto the highway. I'm glad my girls aren't indulging in that type of behavior. Life is too short; make the best out of it while you can. Don't be dependent on a man for nothing. Be your own woman and make your own money, and don't let no man take it from you. If he don't have no drive about his self, or don't take care of his kids, then don't mess with him. Find a man who has the same as you or has more to offer, because he wouldn't be so eager to take, because he knows how it feels to work for his. I see, I said "work for" not "take," strong arm or any other violate shit. Woman, it's okay to give your husband some special treatment. I said *husband,* or if you and your man have been living together for more than two years and you know he loves you and he is taking care of home. Give them some special treatment. I will give you a little of the next book. Say one day you're off and your man has to work, and it's been a struggling time—you've been working late, and he's been working hard between work, the kids, after-school programs. You know, say ya'll haven't been spending much time together, money isn't like it should be, but the bills are paid and food is in the house and no one is in need of anything—treat your man. Make it real romantic. Get some roses (your color doesn't always have to be red—hell, I prefer purple anyways). Get some bubble baths and some beads; get something nice to wear like a sexy bra and panties set—that's all you need—and a robe. Send the kids off somewhere, or tell them, "It's mommy-and-daddy time, so don't knock on the door." When he comes home, feed him a full-course meal, then take him in the room and undress him. Kiss him on the neck at the same time, but get him ready for his bath; while you are undressing him, have the bath water running. As you take his pants off, massage his dick; massage it real gently, but don't let him touch you—make him wait. After that, escort him to the tub and help him get in, then run water over his back with your hands and play with the bubbles. You know, put some of the bubbles on the top of his dick and tell him, "Don't you wish your dick was that big or that long?" (Just kidding, guys, a little humor is always good). After playing with the bubbles, dry him off starting from the back; and as you dry off his body, kiss every section you dry off—remember, he can't touch you. After drying him off, lay him down; and you get on top of him, rubbing his chest. Rub and squeeze at the same time, and suck on the nipples. Men love that shit. It's one of their hot spots. While you're sucking on one nipple, rub the other nipple. Then take your tongue. With one lick, start from the top of his chest and lick all the way down to the navel, but make sure you are licking—start down the middle. Lick around the navel, you should be rubbing both nipples at the same time—and remember, he can't touch you yet. As you start to lick below the navel and you reach the head of the dick . . . to be continued . . . . That's enough. I've given you too much information. But trust me, once you do let him touch you, get ready for the ride, because every fantasy you ever had might just come true if you do it right. See, you have to enjoy life, and don't let everything stress you out. Find something that you like to do, and when you get stressed out, just pick up that hobby. For instance, if you like to work out, when you get stressed out, take it out on those weights. Sex, for instance, if you like having sex, when you get stressed out, you do your damn thang on that dick, then neither one of ya'll will be stressed out anymore. These are lessons I've learned along the way. I didn't do drugs. I used to always fight. But when it came to love, it stressed me out. I was hurting myself the whole time. Hell, he wasn't stressing. While I'm at home crying, asking why, he was out laughing, joking, talking, having a damn good time, and giving my goods to someone else. He wasn't stressing, he was releasing. One thing I did find out is all those times we used to fight, I left marks. He left marks, he always did the same thing, but when I stopped fighting him then cut his ass loose. That man lost his mind. I started playing with his feelings, his emotions, and his heart, like he used to do me. Then I did what he did when I got tired of playing, I just ripped his heart out like he did mine. That is the most hurtful thing you can do to a man. Just don't fuck with him—I'm happy, he's not. I don't have any marks on my body, and he don't have any marks on his body. I'm out with my girls, and he's home alone crying. Because he don't want the boys to see him cry, he makes up an excuse not to go out, hoping I change my mind and come over. NOT! Haha! Love hurts like a bitch, don't it? I hope you enjoy the book. This is my life. Some of it had to be altered to protect the guilty.

Part 1

THE BEGINNING

Chapter 1

When I was fifteen years old, I went to Rickards High School in Tallahassee, Florida. I was in tenth grade. I never was allowed to have a boyfriend. My parents wouldn't let me, and everybody was scared of my brothers, so no one asked me out. I started hanging out with this girl named Shena, and we began to get close. One day, I went to her house, and her cousins from Valdosta, Georgia, were there. I started talking to the cousin Jay on the phone, and we started dating. Jay came to Tallahassee one day when we had a jamboree, and we hooked up that night. He was my first. I was so scared and nervous, but I tried to act as if I had done it before—I was just trying to act grown-up. Well, me trying to be grown up didn't know much about condoms at the time. I got pregnant. First time . . . just my luck. On August 3, 1989, I had a beautiful six-pound, four-ounce baby girl. From then on, my life changed. It all started when I was seventeen years old, back in 1991. I had just graduated from high school. One and a half years later, I was pregnant with my second child. I had gone to Lively Voc-Tech to register for a data-entry program, and I had just taken the entry test to get into the school. I walked outside, and I had seen a classmate; we spoke and caught up on how each of us was doing. Then she told me that her cousin wanted to talk to me. I said if he wanted to talk to me, tell him to come over his self. So she went and told him, and he came over. He came to me with the lamest game I've ever heard. He said, "Hi, my name is Todd, and I'm from New York. I'm twenty-one years old, and I wanted to get to know you." He had this crazy accent, like he didn't have it, but did. I laughed and told him, "Since you made me laugh, I'll give you my number." And it was on from then. I went through hell with that man—from cheating all the time, to getting caught by me when I was four months pregnant with our only son. When I told my parents about him, they didn't like him from jump. My parents weren't too fond of his family, so they didn't want me to date him. Why? I never new. We were back and forth, staying at my parents' house to his family's house. He always kept a job, never mistreated me at the time—I mean, he was like Mr. Perfect in my eyes. So, of course, I stood by my man. I used to always talk to him about his parents. His grandmother from New York raised him. He finally got in touch with his mother. He hadn't seen his mother in over ten years. They talked, and he talked to his stepfather about me and him moving to Navarre, Florida, right next to Fort Walton Beach, Florida. His mother and stepfather said it was okay; and that following week, they came and picked us up from the store down the street from my parents' house. Todd had two stepbrothers named Nick and Ryan. Nick was two and Ryan was ten. I was trying to take my oldest daughter with me, but my parents had put her in their room and wouldn't let me get her, and Todd's parents were coming. My parents and I had this big fallout, and they asked us to leave, so we left. When his parents arrived, we gave them gas money and left. We stayed up there for about one month before his mother started flipping out. His mother had some serious issues, and she was so quick to fight her husband, it didn't make any sense. But his stepdad never hit her when we were there; he took all the licks. We paid her $180 for rent for the both of us and all of my food stamps. One day, Todd and Ryan were arguing, and his stepmother took Ryan's side of jump. I was in the room when they were arguing, and Todd was working the night shift at Winn Dixie 10:00 p.m.-7:00 a.m. Todd came in the room to cool down, and his mother came in the room and told us to get out. Todd hit the roof, and I didn't blame him. We had just given her rent and all of our food stamps; we had just bought a red station wagon for $200. The car had ants in it and little holes in the bottom of the floor, but it wasn't too bad. And on top of that, I was eight months pregnant, and it was hot. We had no money, but she kept saying, "All I see is your father. I need you to leave, I don't want ya'll here." I mean, she just flipped out. His stepfather tried to talk to her, but she just cursed him out and tried to fight him, so we left. For a whole week, we slept in that car. When Todd went to work at night, I would sleep in the car in the parking lot, and on his breaks, he would bring me something to eat and check up on me. Then when he got off, we would drive to a gas station so we could wipe off, then we drove to the park and then he went to sleep. When he got paid, he put me on a bus back to my parents, and one week later he came too. At the time, my parents were okay with it, until he got there. Then three days later, my mom started tripping, so he found another job that required him to travel—a door-to-door salesman. At first, I kept faking that I was in labor, because I didn't want him to go; then the day after he left, I had my baby—which was on his birthday. He was too happy; she was seven pounds, six ounces—my biggest child. About two weeks later, he came home, and my parents were too mad about that. We stayed at my parents' house for about two months, then we moved into our own place. That's when everything really changed; he started being real possessive. I mean he would go to work and I was a stay-at-home mom. The house stayed clean, he always had a hot meal, and I would have his clothes out for him and his bath water ready. This was the first time I ever lived with a boy, so I was too excited. I remember 1992 was the first time I ever took a drink, and Todd got me drunk for the first time. All I did was laugh. Todd started laughing, asking me what was so funny. I couldn't answer him—because first off I didn't know, and second I couldn't stop laughing to answer him. He was the first man to ever go down on me, and he was the first person I ever went down on to.

I would be sitting on the porch, talking to my neighbors (females), and he would go inside the house and flick the porch lights on and off, and it was daytime. My neighbors would say, "Tasha, you know what that means—time to go in the house." I would go in, and we would argue. At that time, he didn't put his hands on me. We would just argue. We would invite his family over to play cards or do something. One day, his cousins came over (the same one that introduced us), and we were just having a get-together. Todd and I were arguing about something, and he hit me in my face. I was so shocked, but before I knew it, I pushed him into the wall, and when he stepped up, there was a big hole in the wall. I guess I had hurt his pride in front of his cousin and her boyfriend, so of course we fought. They broke it up, and we made love that night, and everything was cool.

It was a Friday night. I was hot-curling my hair because I was going out, and Todd was going out with his friends. Todd didn't want me to go, so he started an argument with me; and he got mad because I wasn't entertaining him, and he hit me in my left jaw, and I got my hot curlers and burned him down his arm and pushed him down the stairs after—we didn't have any more fights for a while. About six months later, Todd's cousin came to the house just to chill with us, and Todd and I got into it again, because I wanted to go out. He jumped on me, and his cousin had called their step uncle, Roy (who was married to their aunt and he was my cousin). Roy came over to see what was going on. I told him I wanted Todd to leave. I wanted him to watch him pack his stuff and escort him out of our home. Roy said okay, but instead, Roy took Todd to jail. He said he had a warrant in New York, so he went to jail. I waited a couple of days before I went to see him, plus I didn't have a car at the time. He apologized to me and we kept talking, and he asked me to move to New York and marry him. I was so shocked and happy, and. like a dumbass, I said yes and did just that. We eloped and got married October 21, 1992. I left everything in the apartment, and my kids and I moved. All we had were our clothes. We got a neighbor to take us to the bus station, and we were on our way to Riverhead Long Island, New York. When I got there, I was so amazed, because I only had seen New York on TV. His grandmother (his mother's mother) had picked us up from the bus station and took me around New York for a minute. We had stopped at this place called Roy Rogers, and I had talked with the manager and asked him if they were hiring. He said yes, so I filled out an application and got the job and started the very next day. I was like, *Damn! First day here and already got a job.* So I was working and living with his grandparents, and everything was cool. She introduced me to her friends, but she wouldn't let me go anywhere without her. Then we had already worked out an agreement over the phone about how much I was going to pay, then when I got there, she went up on the price. Daughter like mother. I had found me a babysitter, but then I found out the babysitter was on crack, so I had to quit my job. I was so mad 'cause I was about to become a manager. Plus I used to walk in the snow to get to work, which was about four miles from where I was staying. Thank God, one of the managers had told me about their old apartment, and I talked to the landlord, and he let me rent it for $500 a month. It was a three-story house. Someone stayed on the third floor and the middle, and I stayed in the basement. I was getting $757 a month—$289 a month for food stamps, and I lived off of $257 a month in cash and the food stamps with two kids for seven months. I had one child in diapers, and my eldest was three years old at the time. Times were so hard, but I did it. I used to travel six hours to see Todd upstate, and I had to pay $75, so I visited him once every two months. Todd had two weeks left before he was getting out when I started my nursing class. He came home, and everything was good for about two weeks. He started changing; he was already seeing this other girl, and had a get-out-of-jail party in her basement. We were fussing again—like, usually at his party, when these guys got into it and would threaten each other, and one left and said he would be back. Well, the guy came back with a bulletproof vest on and was high as a kite on cocaine. He had just started shooting, so we all were running everywhere. Then as I looked up, he was next to me; then I saw about six bullets hitting him, and he was still standing until one of those guys shot him in the head, and he fell. I had never seen anyone get shot, let alone die, before. I'm looking like, *Ooh shit, is this real.* Then I heard some yelling—and it was Todd's friend—so we hopped in someone's car and took him to the hospital. Todd gave this lame excuse for not coming home, and I left. I had class in the morning, and I was still in shock. I had started hanging out with this girl in my class named Sabrina. She had a car. She would pick me up from school and take me to the store; she would just help me out. One Sunday, the same girl whose place he had his party at came to my house with my friend Sabrina, and she knocked on the door. I opened it, and she started telling me that Todd said he wanted to be with her and that he was leaving me and that they were having sex—I mean all kind of shit. Todd came from the room, cursing them out; then I confronted him in front of her, and, of course, he lied. When they left, that man shocked the hell out of me. I ran out the house and up the steep driveway and across the street. Tisa was in the house, sleeping. My oldest was in Florida at the time. He ran after me, grabbed me by my hair, and started dragging me back across the street. People were watching, but no one would help me. I was even yelling *help*! They just stood there. I was crying, kicking, and screaming. As he was dragging me down the hill, I had grabbed a hold of the fence that went all the way down the driveway. He pulled me until my fingers let go. Then he grabbed my feet, and my face was now on the concrete, and he was dragging me down the hill. My face was hitting the ground. I somehow turned on my back, and my back got scraped up. When we got in the house, he beat me like crazy, then locked me in the house. From that moment, I was afraid of my husband. The next day, it was time for me to go to school, and he told me that I wasn't allowed to go to school. I wasn't allowed to leave the house, so my friend Sabrina went and got my teachers, and they came. When they came, he opened the door. We all talked, but I didn't tell them what happened. But they could see. I went to school, and they cheered me up. I even graduated with a good grade. Nevertheless, time went on. Todd started taking the rent money, and went partying, staying out for weeks, and leaving us at home with no food or money. He just didn't give a shit about us. All he was worrying about was his self. Until one day, we were sitting down, watching TV, when all of a sudden, he just pulled my hair back for no reason and started hitting me. I didn't do anything. I was in the house all day, playing with my baby, and he just started hitting me. After he beat me, he told me to fix dinner, and I did. As I was cooking, I noticed a box in the back of the cabinet. I grabbed it—it was rat poison. I looked at him to see what he was doing, and I put four pebbles on the counter and hid the box. I had fixed some spaghetti for us, and then after I fixed our plates, I had chopped up the poison real small and mixed it in his spaghetti and gave it to him. After that, I went and got my plate after I saw him take the first bite. I didn't have much of an appetite, because my throat was sore from him choking me. I was feeding my baby and eating real slow to see what was going to happen to him; then afterwards, he said he was tired and sleepy. Then he went to sleep. I was so nervous and scared, I didn't know what to do. I had no phone, no money, and no way of getting home. My parents had blocks on their phones. I was just stuck like chuck, and I didn't think about that at the time, so I waited to see if he would wake up. I'll be damned, he woke up. About two hours later, he went back to sleep. This lasted for one full week, Todd kept saying, "What is wrong with me? Why do I keep going to sleep like this?" and then he would doze off. I'm reading the warning signs on the box, saying to myself, *Why won't this motherfucker die?* I realize that it didn't work, so when Todd went back to sleep, I got some super glue, pulled his pants down, and started rubbing him. He moved a little, but he didn't get up. I got the super glue and glued his dick to his thigh, then glued his pee hole up so he couldn't pee. About one hour later, Todd woke up and said, "What the fuck?" and looked down and realized he couldn't pee. That boy hollered like a girl. I pushed him down on the floor. He reached for the phone, and I snatched it out the wall—even though the phone was off, you still could call 911. Then I started kicking him, until I kicked his ass out the door. He ran up the hill to the pay phone and called 911. They came and took him to the hospital. I went to the hospital to see what was going on, and the doctors were laughing so hard, they were crying. It was so funny. He looked up and saw me and told me he was going to kill me. I politely held up the super glue and said, "Now what are you going to do to me?" He just lay back down and waited for them to do surgery on him. Boy, did that feel good. The following week, it was the first. I had told Todd I was going back home, because it was too cold and I was tried of struggling. He told me he was going too. I told him he would be a fool if he did, and he did. We got on the Greyhound and were heading back to Florida; it was a two-day ride on the bus. He was trying to talk to me on the bus, but I wouldn't say anything to him. He didn't like that, so he grabbed me by my neck again and told me not even think about leaving him or try to get home and show out. He said he would find me and kill me if I tried anything, and I believed him. Hell, I got enough ass beating, and I was scared of him; so when we got to Tallahassee, I didn't say anything. My parents were cool with it for a minute, 'cause they wanted me home, so they let him stay for about two months, then Mom started tripping again. I had gotten me an apartment in the projects, and we moved in together again. This time, things were a lot different. I mean, things were happening real fast. Todd had stopped putting his hands on me, and he was making money. I mean so much money, I was scared to even spend it. Todd was bringing home at least $3,000 to $4,000 a week, and I had a good job with the state. It was all good, until he found some new friends; and he wanted to be a player like his friends, except his friends weren't married—Todd was, and we started fussing and fighting again. One night, I told Todd I didn't want him to go out. I was mad as hell 'cause he had been gone for three days and then he comes home go to sleep, wake up, watch a little TV, then try and bounce again; and I told him, if he left, to not bring his ass back. He flipped out, "Ooh, you kicking me out?" I told him, "Hell yeah." This was not a pit stop. He hit me. I hit his ass back in the face, then I tried to kick him in his nuts, but he didn't feel a thing. He grabbed me by my neck, threw me down, and started choking me until I could hardly breathe. Then he started choking me with one hand, took his other hand, and put it in my mouth—his fingers were in my throat. I just knew I was going to die. I had started feeling real light-headed, and I felt my eyes rolling in the back of my head, then he finally let me up and left. That time, I was so glad when he left and didn't come back for a week. I used to tell him that if he didn't start spending time with me, someone else would. I had been telling him this for a while. He acted as if he didn't care, so I started going out and meeting other people and enjoying myself. He used to tell me to go ahead, and that I was ugly; nobody didn't want an already-made family, so good luck. For a long time, I believed that and would just sit home and cry, while he was out doing his thing. A year had passed, and Todd was being Todd. I was hanging with my brother's girlfriend a lot, because she used to help me keep my mind off my husband. Todd had called me on my cell phone, sounding all nice and sweet, asking me what time was I going to be home. And I told him I was going to be home in an hour—I was already on my way home. Then he said he would be there when I got home. I said okay; then he said he loved me, and I told him I loved him too. I knew right then something was up, so I pulled into the complex and then into the parking lot. Whom should I see coming out of the house but this girl getting out of the driver's side of a car getting into the passenger side. I just stopped and looked at Todd, and Todd saw me, kept on walking, got into the driver's side of the car, got in, and went to back up. The parking lot is one way in and one way out, and I was blocking the entry. So what do I do? I hit that bitch car a couple of times. Todd finally got away, and then I grabbed my baby and went into the house and started getting his shit out of my house. About thirty minutes later, he called me, telling me what he was going to do to me and that I messed him up with this so-called meeting he had. All lies. I told him to kiss my ass, because he didn't have a key to the top lock; and it was locked, so he couldn't get in. I called my brother's girlfriend and told her what happen and that I was going to kill him. So my brother, his girlfriend, and his girlfriend's cousin came over. I let them in, and Todd said, "I will leave. Just let me get my clothes." I told him, "HELL NO!" So he hung up the phone, and about ten minutes later, he was at the bottom of the steps, calling my name. I opened my door, and we started fussing. He came upstairs and into the house. My brother was trying to keep the peace, but all I wanted to do was hurt him, so I grabbed a butcher knife and tried to stave him, but my brother got in the way. Then I pushed him out the door and locked it. Todd went back downstairs and started yelling again. Then I opened the door again. This time, I started throwing his things outside on the ground. Boy, was he hot. He was having a fit. He called his friend to come and pick him up, then he left. After that, we split up. He got his own place, and I stayed at mine. Of course, we still were having sex. Then I started missing him, and I wanted him to come back, but he wouldn't. I said, "Okay cool." A month later, I had gotten real sick to a point where I had to be admitted into the hospital. I found out I was pregnant with my third child. "Damn, damn, damn" is all I could say, because I was not expecting that. I had to stay in the hospital for one week. I called Todd and told him I was pregnant and that there could be a chance I'd lose the baby down the line and asked if he wanted me to keep the baby. That bitch said he didn't care, then hung up on me. Not once did he come to the hospital to see me or call to check up on me—nothing. Only my brother's girlfriend, family, and this one guy I was seeing. We never had sex, but he was crazy about me. I told him I was pregnant, and he didn't have a problem with that. He brought me fruits, flowers, and candy. He even drove me home from the hospital. About two days later, there was a knock at the door, and it was Todd and his friend. I barely opened my door. He looked at me as though I was crazy. Todd told me to let him in. I told him no and to never come back. He asked, "Why? 'Cause you got somebody in there?" in a joking way, then started laughing. So I opened the door a little wider, just enough for him to see my friend, and my friend didn't have a shirt on. Then he busted into the house, and his friend grabbed him. My friend had gone into the back room and put on a shirt, which was Todd's. Hell, I didn't know. Then Todd went to throw a chair, but my daughter had come into the kitchen where we were. Todd was like, "Okay." I said, "I told you that I was getting lonely, and you were always gone. Hell, I'm lying in the hospital with your baby, and you never called, came by, or nothing. So FUCK YOU! Then I slammed my door, and damn that felt good. Down the line, I broke up with the guy and just chilled. Todd popped up at the house again, and this time, he was by his self, and he had a different attitude. He was much nicer, and I could see that he was hurt, but I didn't give a damn; I didn't care. We started talking about the past—the good things that we did. Laughing and things. I was lying on my back, on the sofa, and he was sitting on the couch. He came over to where I was and lay on me and was telling me he was sorry and all this crazy stuff, then he asked me if I had ever slept with anyone. I told him yes. He leaned up and looked me into my eyes and asked me again, and I told him yes, without a care in the world. He pulled out his gun, put it to my head, and said, "I'm going to ask you one more time. Did you sleep with anyone else besides me?" And I said, "HELL YES!" He looked at me and said, "Are you serious?" I told him yes, and then he asked me how many times. I told him it was none of his business—it was only one time. Hey, what can I say? I need a quick fix, and I sure as hell got one, and it was worth it. Todd got up and left, then he called me later on that night and said, "I think I'm going to go ahead and give you your divorce." And I said thank you and hung up the phone. I didn't call him anymore. I had started moving on with my life, getting ready for the baby. Then two days later, Todd came calling me, telling me he couldn't live without me and he wanted to make it work and all kinds of stuff. I was tired of all the bullshit. Like one time, Todd went to a club called the Moon; and at that time, I didn't go out, but I decided to go out. It was me and my brother's girlfriend. Soon, as I walked into the door, who do I see all in a whore's face? Todd. He looked at me as though he saw a ghost, and we were married. None of his friends knew he was married. We went on the dance floor, and that slick bastard spun me around on the dance floor, then disappeared. So after the club had closed, the parking lot was thick. Then my brother's girlfriend saw Todd before I did, and she said "Ooh, Todd, your wife is right here." He first tried to duck down in the seat, but I had already seen him. By the time he turned around to see where I was, I had him by his collar, and I told the girl who was driving, "If you say anything, I'll bash your fuckin' head in." She didn't say shit. At first, he tried to act all grand, so I told him he was cancelled. I totted my ass up, and I was switching, walking away. Many men tried to holler, so I hollered back. Here comes Todd, grabbing me, yelling "Hell naw! This is my wife!" grabbing me all over. So I pushed him away, then he wanted to fight me. My brother's girlfriend saw a beer bottle, and she had grabbed it and told him to hit me if he wanted to. Me and my brother's girlfriend got into my car and bounced.

Todd had moved out and gotten his own place, but we were still having sex. And one day, on my lunch break, I went to Todd's new apartment. We were talking and ended up having sex. Do you know this SOB told me after we had sex that he didn't want to be bothered anymore? I started ripping his place apart, I said, "How could you have sex with me then say that? You are a cold-hearted BITCH! I'm your wife!"

One night, I was going to go out, but I stayed at home, thinking about Todd; and then I got a phone call around 2:30 a.m., and it was my brother.

He said "Sis, what are you doing?" I told him, "Just watching TV." He said, "You are not going to believe this shit. Todd just blew the horn at me, waving, with another girl in the car." I said, "You're lying." He was like, "Naw, Sis, I'm dead serious. You need to leave him alone. If he don't have any respect for you, then you don't need him." My brother said, "What kind of man blows at his wife's brother with another female with him? Todd don't give two cents about you." So I called Todd and asked him where he was. He told me he'd gone to his spot. I asked him if that girl was with him. He said, "Yeah, did your brother tell you?" I told him, "What the fuck do you think?" Then I said, "You know, you are a cold-hearted fucker, and you are going to get what is coming to you," then hung up. I thought about it and got in my car and went to his place, but before I got there, I saw a big brick and took it with me. I sat there in my car for about ten minutes, thinking about all the shit he did to me. I got out of my car and threw the brick in his front-room window, then left. Todd called me and was cursing me out. I just laughed and hung up. Todd called me the next day, sounding all nice. He said he deserved that, but I had made him mad, and he wanted to get back at me. I asked him, "So how did your date go?" He told me she left. I didn't believe him, because I know how he is—she probably did leave, but not before he got him some. After all that, I took him back.

Part 2

WHAT IN THE HELL WAS I THINKING?

I went through hell with that man, from cheating all the time to getting caught by me when I was four months pregnant with our only son. Todd was doing two years in prison, and I was waiting on him faithfully. He had a baby the same age as our son. My son's birthday is June 15, 2001—seven pounds, two ounces—and the child he made on me is November 14, 2001. Ain't that a BITCH! I knew the bitch when we were staying in Todd's apartment. The bitch stayed upstairs, six apartments down on the same side. He got arrested in Port St. Joe, and I had to go get my car and check on him. She took me, then turned around and fucked my husband. She was so quiet, but you know what they say—those quite ones are the ones you have to watch. On top of that, she got pregnant. This is one of the reasons why I ask myself, "Is he worth it?"

Here is another reason: I came home late one day from work. Todd and I got into a big fight the night before; I didn't want to have sex and he made me, and I was pregnant, so I just lay there the whole time he was fucking me. I was complaining so much of how nasty it felt and how nasty he was to be out there screwing all those different females then come home to me and want to have sex with me. I complained so much, until he couldn't take it no more and he stopped. He got up, cursed me out, then went into the shower. And I guess he relieved himself and called some girl to pick him up from down the street. One hour later, I went to work—my hours were from 10:00 p.m. till 7:00 a.m., and I was a CSM at Wal-Mart. I thought about it all night long (oh yeah, the fight was about him cheating and staying out all the time, not coming home—of course, he kept denying it), and I said I was going to make it up to him. We were going to go to church, and I would cook a good Sunday meal, and we would eat, make love, and then talk. So then after I got off from work, I bought him a tie and a shirt, and I bought myself a pair of stockings. While I was shopping, I starting having these funny feelings. Something kept saying, *Put the shit down and go home.* I shook it off, then I had a vision for your ass—I had a vision of Todd having sex with another girl in my house. I just shook it off, I started shopping again; then about five minutes later, another vision came to me, and it was the same thing. I finally said, "Let me take my ass home," so I paid for the stuff then went home. Got there, there was a car in the driveway I had never seen before (mind you, I'm saying to myself he wouldn't do that to me, shaking it off). I blocked the car in, but not enough. I left everything in the car. As I went into the driveway, I was looking in the old white car, and I see hair waves in the back seat and female things. I closed the car door real softly, got the house keys out, and put the rest of the keys in my hand so they wouldn't rattle. I walked up the steps real quiet, stuck the key in the door, and snatched the door open quickly. "WHAT THE FUCK!" was all I could say. I saw him naked, trying to run, and she was on the floor naked. They were fucking, and the position she was in, she could see my wedding pictures. She sat up and was holding the cover over her, saying she didn't know. Bitch, please, you knew. I went straight to the kitchen and got a big-ass knife; and he went grabbing his dick, she tried to put her clothes on. "The HELL YOU ARE! Get the FUCK OUT, and take your clothes with you in your hand." She ran out of my house naked. I locked my door and went straight to his ass. He ran in the bathroom, so I went in after him—and there's not a whole lot of space there, and he knew how I am about being closed in. He shut the door and locked it. We were tussling over the knife (I'm seven months pregnant with my son). He got it, then started saying some crazy shit like, "If you ain't going to be with me, then you won't be with anyone else. I will kill you first!" The look I had on my face, I was like, "Let's do this." So I started hitting first. I fault him. He was trying to hold me down till I calmed down—which was in about forty-five minutes. As I was calming down, I started thinking, *Okay I'll calm down, I'm only going to play your game so I can get the hell out of the bathroom.* He apologized to me, but what was the ass kicker is he said, "Let's go to church." Now you should have seen the look on my face. This asshole was tripping for real. I laughed and said, "Okay." We went to a friend's church—about seven to eight members, including the pastor and his wife. "Good People." They had altar call, and he went up there and said he had done wrong by his wife and he wanted to be saved again. I said to myself I knew the hell he didn't. Everybody started praising the Lord; they were happy, and they started talking about forgiveness. All I could do was say, "Lord, I love you. I do want to do good by you, I want to change, but not this time. Lord, please forgive me. I'm not ready to forgive this son of a bitch. Not this time." Everyone went to hug him, shaking his hand; you know how they do it when someone gets saved. Then I'm the last one he turned to, everyone was looking at me. He held his arms out to me and said, "I'm really sorry for what I've done, will you please forgive me?" I looked at him straight in his eyes and turned and walked out without a word. That man had crossed the line. How in the hell are you going to use God on me? Punk, you fucked up, that's all to it. Most of my feelings were gone instantly. We went home. We didn't say anything to each other that night, so what does he do? Get dressed, call another ho, and got out; and he didn't come home until the next day—in the afternoon, around 3:00 p.m. I didn't say a word. Hell, I didn't care anymore, but he wouldn't leave for good, so I decided not to pay any more bills in the house. It was my first house I was trying to buy, and this shit had messed it up. I didn't work as much anymore; we had to move. We moved in with my friend named Keisha. She is a character for you. I know I will never meet anyone like her. Here we go.

Part 3

THE ROUGH MOVE

Keisha is the type of person who will help anyone with no questions asked, but if you fall out with her, she will let everyone know she helped you. She goes to church faithfully, but if you did the things she did, you would go all the time too. Don't get me wrong, she really was trying to change her life and she does have a heart of gold, but some things are just in you. When I met Keisha, it was on a workday and I was pregnant with my son, and she just clicked with me. Plus, she new the business in the streets, you best believe if she got a problem with you, she will go to you and tell you and not give a damn what you think. Can she fight? I heard it both ways, can I verify? No. I've never seen her fight; no one would fight her. Anyways, after I caught Todd and we were on bad terms (Todd and I), I let the house note go; and Keisha let me, Todd, and my two kids move in with her, her husband, her five children, and her nephew. She lived in a beautiful four-bedroom, two-bath, two-story house (Keisha had four boys and one girl). I had two girls and a boy on the way. We stayed there; my parents came to see me in the hospital. I had my only son. Todd had his leg in a cast, he could hardly work. He worked at a car wash with that cast on his leg. After I had my son, things changed. I remember it was three weeks after I had my son, and it was raining and everybody went outside to play in the rain, except Todd and Keisha's husband. We were barefoot and running up and down the street, acting like little kids. Nevertheless, I got real sick and was back in the hospital. I went outside too early. We stayed all cooped up in the room, and Keisha didn't like that. So, of course, everyone knew what happened, and we were living with her. I was ready to go to my parents' house. Todd had violated his probation; it was all a mess.

Let me take you back to my house before I moved out. Keisha was there at my house on May 19, 2001. It was my daughter Tisa's and Todd's birthdays, and I had a little something for the both of them at the house. So a friend of mine named Plyshette (who was Keisha's sister) brother wanted to talk to me. He was in jail facing life for pimping underage girls. I have three girls. What the FUCK! I looked as if I was trying to holler back at him. He mailed me a letter, and it had the wrong name on it, so I looked at it and told my daughter to put the letter back and put the flag up for the mailman. The next day, Kelly brought the mail in. When I looked at it later on that night, it was the same letter, so I threw it in the room unopened and forgot to put it in the mailbox. Todd found the letter on his birthday. Keisha and I had gone to the store, and when we got back, he was talking crazy (now I remind you he had just got caught with a girl in my house), so I overlooked what he was saying. Then he said something that really pissed me off. He said, "I know I hurt you, but if you're going to talk to someone, get someone better. Not someone who is facing life." I went off. I told him, "You son of a bitch, what the fuck is your problem? What in the hell are you talking about? Just say it, because you're pissing me off." I was about eight months pregnant. He jumped up and threw me the letter. So it went on from then. Keisha and her husband were trying to keep us from fighting, so Keisha and I went to the porch to cool off. We're outside talking and here comes Mr. Todd talking to me and saying, "I'm sorry. I was wrong, but why him?" I went off again, and we had a deck porch and one of the boards were loose, so I kicked that bitch one good time in the right spot and the whole board came undone. I got that board and wore his back out. Keisha and her husband had to get it from me. Todd had no job at the time—lost his family and home, all because he wasn't taking care of home. So after that, we all went to Keisha's house, the kids went upstairs doing there own thing, and the grown ups played spade and talked shit. (My car was broken down at the time, so I had no ride either.) Despite that, we had a good time, then I got sleepy, went home, and he still didn't get any loving on his birthday.

Part 4

DRAMA

Chapter 2

It's the year 2002. Junior and I were staying at my mother's. U.S. marshalls arrested Todd from my mother's house. We knew it was going to happen. It was just a matter of time. He was working, trying to make sure I was going to be okay. He had Junior everywhere he went. It was kind of cute seeing him play daddy. He goes away for two years, and I wait on him faithfully. I was working two jobs, doing what I had to do to take care of my four children. I was working double shifts on the weekend out of town just so I could visit him. I was working from 3:00 p.m. to 7:00 a.m., going to see him for about three hours, then going home, trying to get some rest as well as spend time with my family, then do it all over again. I moved my family into this two-story house in a nice neighborhood, so he could have a nice home to come home to. He got out and everything was okay until I found out about this secret he had been keeping from me for two years—basically the whole time he was locked up. We started having problems with the landlord, so we moved back to Panama City, Florida. And this asshole got worse. Cheating wasn't the word for it. He dogged me so bad, until every feeling I ever had for him was completely gone—it had left. There was nothing left in me to love him anymore—between making a baby and getting caught with another girl in my house. I was tired! One day, we were in Panama City, Florida, looking for a place to stay, and he was driving; and I was on the passenger side, looking through his papers, looking for something. I saw a paper that had IRS on it, and he was looking funny. I didn't take a good look at it, so I said, "You better file your taxes before they get you." Todd was like, "I know." Then I flip back to it, 'cause I knew I had seen a name, so I said, "Wait a minute," then started reading it—then he tried to grab it from me. I saw another female's name on it, then I read *child support*. I didn't even look up at him; I just punched him in his jaw while he was driving. Then I read the birthday on it. I really flipped the strip. I went off. All I could think about was I waited on him faithfully, and he knew and never said one word to me. Then he said he had to take a DNA test, but I knew better. I knew he took one while he was in jail. So I went along with it—why, I don't know. The next week, he had to go to the Child Support Office. He claimed to get the results. He knew it was his. When he came out of the office, I said, "It's yours, isn't it?" He said yes. I said, "I'm done." No more sex from me, and that drove him crazy. He used to say, "That's a shame. I can't even get any sex from my own wife." I would say, "Yeap, I don't want it no more, it's nasty to me now. Too many females had you." One thing about me, no one else has had it; and I want to test the waters, and I knew I wouldn't have any problems doing so, because too many men already wanted me—and he knew that. One time, he went to jail for running his much so much. I made him sit there for a minute, because the night he left me to go to the club, we had a big fight and he stole some money from me and left, then cursed me out. It wasn't the first time he stole money from me. He had gone out and made some money one time, then turned around and gambled all of his money away, but he knew the next morning he had to go to child support court. He strong-armed me, took my money, then made me dress up in my uniform and go to court with him. That money was for the lights. I told him, "Once I do this, there will be a price." He was going to have to pay, because no one strong-arms me and gets away with it. I told him that the next time he went to jail—which I know he was going to eventually do—I wasn't going to get him out, and that's exactly what I did. Made his ass sit and took myself shopping with the money I could have used to get his sorry ass out. That morning, he wasn't home. Usually, he's home before the kids have to go to school. It was the first day of school; and Tisa had to walk to school, Junior was a car rider, and Kelly road the bus. Kelly got on the bus, no Todd. I walked Tisa to school came back home, no Todd. I walked Junior to school, no Todd. I'm walking home mad as hell, and then I get a phone call from him. He is in jail; someone got shot at the club and died. He was drunk and saying "people know their rights" and all kinds of shit. Why would you be talking shit when you're dirty? You would be quiet I would think, but no, not Mr. Todd. He has all the sense. He kept on talking after the officers asked him to be quiet. Then finally, they got fed up with him and threw him against the van and arrested him and searched him and found two small bags of weed—and he was on probation. Now he's violated again, so I made him sit there for a minute and started testing the waters. Boy, look a hear, let's just say *nice* . . . I never knew I would get so much attention. I mean, men were showing me so much love left and right, without me giving up anything. That's what I'm talking about—much love. Todd kept calling the club where I worked at collect. That boy burned that phone up, because I was never home, and I told the children not to answer his calls. He can't help pay for it, and he wants me to get him out. He better sit down somewhere and just deal with it. For the first time, I can say I was in control, and it felt damn good. After that, I got called up for Iraq. Now isn't this some shit? I'm finally happy and I get called up, and I graduated from college in May, but I needed two more credits to get my AA degree in paralegal. Someone called me from the unit, telling me I had one week to pack up and go. I took my kids to my mother's house and went back and cleaned up my house. I brought my oldest brother, Mac, and my little sister, Tina, back with me. Tina is my ace coon boom; she is my heart. I don't know what I would do if anything ever happened to my little sis. They helped me move, and my brother also helped himself to Todd's clothes. As I was getting ready for Iraq, I went and got my shots and everything in order. Then they turned around and told me I had two weeks before I would leave. I was so pissed, I had put everything in storage, took my kids to my parents, and I didn't have anywhere to stay. So I ended up staying on the base and working at the club. Todd finally got out, and I told my sister to give him the keys to his storage, 'cause I had two storages—one with me and my kids' stuff in it, and the other one had his clothes and everything else in the house. I didn't want anything. I just wanted to be done with him. All we did was fight mainly, because I wouldn't give him any sex.

I remember one time, when I was working at Sears and he came home real late, I mean I was late for work. Todd and I were fussing, and he put his hands on me; and we were fighting, and this time, it was in front of the kids. We were fighting, and we ended up outside. I ended up on the ground, and he was on top of me, trying to choke me, and I had seen a writing pen on the ground. I picked it up and just started stabbing him at his chest. He had a bunch of little holes in him. My daughter Tisa got scared and called 911. All they'd seen was me stabbing him, and I hit him with a brick. They came in the backyard and asked Todd if he wanted to press charges on me. I had an "I don't care" attitude. I went to the back of the police car and told them to take me. Hell, if this is what it takes to get away from him, then I'm ready to go. Todd told them I was stressing, because I got called up to go to Iraq and I was scared. I told the police, "Bullshit. I'm tired of this man, and he can't make me be with him, and please take me to jail." Well, they apologized to me and wished me luck and told us no more fighting, especially in front of the kids.

Any hoot, he finally got out. He somehow got the key to my storage and took my gun. He was speeding, and the police were after him. He called me on the cell phone (I was on my way to Mississippi for training, getting ready to go to Iraq) and told me the police were after him. I told him, "If you have anything in the car, throw it out. And if you have anything on you, get rid of it too." Then the phone cut off. I lost the signal. Then the phone rang again. He told me he was about to go to jail. I said, "No really, dumbass—you're running from the police." I asked him where was he at, and he told me he was under a trailer. Then the next thing I heard was dogs barking, and he said they let the dogs out on him, then my phone went dead. I didn't hear from him again, then when we got to a rest stop. I used another sargeant's phone and called the jail. They had him. Dumbass had weed in the ashtray and my gun. He's out on bond, and he was at "three strikes you're out." Everything was a mess. I explained to the prosecutor that it was my gun and that I left it in the car by accident, so I stopped him from getting life. I took the hit on the gun. Todd got four years. He was lucky, because the asshole was out on two bonds. Off to Iraq I went.

Part 5

THE GOOD TIMES

Now Todd and I did have some good times—our first apartment, getting drunk for the first time, when we were staying in Holton Street despite the other stuff he did. When I did take him back and he realized that he had another baby on the way and he didn't want anyone else raising his child, he stepped his game up. I mean, Todd and the landlord did not get along, and she told me that he couldn't stay with me; and then she told Todd that if he really loved me, he would move me from the projects. She then told him that she didn't think he could do that. She told him that he wasn't a real man. I don't know if what she said made him step his game up or if he really wanted the best for me and the children, so he really shocked me. Todd started bringing home some real money. Then one day, Todd didn't come home and didn't call. I called his cell phone, and he didn't answer. So about three hours later, I get a phone call from his friend named Luke. Luke said, "Don't worry, baby girl. T-Lo is okay. He came into some money, and I needed to hide him out for a minute." I'm thinking to myself, *What is going on?* Then Todd finally called me and explained to me what was going on. Todd told me that he had to lie low for a couple of days, then he would be home. I was worried because of what he had told me. Then he came home on the third day. It was early, he had these guys lined up, and he had a U-Haul. I was like, "Todd, what are you doing?" He said, "I'm moving you and our kids out of these projects," and he moved us in two hours. The only thing we took were our clothes, dishes, pictures, and other little items. We left the bedroom set and the furniture there. Todd paid our rent up for six months, furnished the whole house. I mean, everything was paid for in the house, fixed up my car and his car, then put money in my account. I can say he did the damn thang. About three months ago, my brother Mac and Todd had beat up this boy that my brother knew; his sister had a baby from my other brother K. We all went to school together, and everybody was cool. Mac had been beating this boy up for sometime now, and the boy got tired of it and shot my brother twice in the leg. Then he went after Todd. When he would see Todd, he pulled a gun out on him, stole his car, parked it in the back of the projects, and stole the system out of it. Todd called me and told me what happen, so I went to the projects and got the car. This went on for a while. Todd got tired of it and decided to do something about it the next time he saw him. Todd and Luke were riding through French town; I was at home. As they were riding, Luke told Todd, "There goes that nigga right there." Todd told Luke to take him back to the house. Todd came in and told me he would be right back, not knowing what this nut was going to do. Todd had Luke park across the street, around the corner. It was around one thirty in the afternoon on Halloween Day. After riding through Frenchtown again, they spotted the same person. Luke parked the car, and Todd got out and went across the street and emptied his 9mm clip on the boy, shooting the boy all in his vital sign (the boy lived). Then he ran back across the street, got into the car, and bucked. (Some of this is true, and some you can use your imagination.) Todd came home and got rid of everything that looked like what he had on, the weapon, and bullets. He still hadn't told me what had happened. We went over to our friend's house. The girl was pregnant too. We all went out to eat at Ryan's. That night, we went to my parents' house to take the kids trick-or-treating. Todd got a phone call from his uncle telling him he heard that Todd had shot somebody in Frenchtown. I looked, and Todd told him it wasn't him; and he told his uncle he didn't need to be spreading rumors about that because it wasn't true. About three days went by. I was at work, and I wasn't at my desk when Todd called. I checked my voice mail. At first, I didn't understand it so, I played it again, and all I heard was, "Get down on the floor, put the phone down." I left work in a hurry; when I got home, they were searching the house. I asked to see the search warrant. Then this nasty lady cop was smiling and saying, "Yeah, we got your boy." So the lady cop and I got into it. She said, "If you keep talking, I'll take you to jail too." I told her, "Do it, so I can get paid." Then a male officer came and talked to me outside. I asked, "Why is the video camera on the ground?" I thought you couldn't search anyone's home unless someone was there; and if no one was there, it had to be videotaped. He agreed and said they had already videotaped what they needed to. They tore up my apartment, and all they found was two bullets with no fingerprints. They found bullet shells at the scene. No finger prints. If it were me, I would have wiped off the bullets as I loaded the gun. They had nothing on him. They found a gun outside of the apartment—it wasn't the right gun, and it was outside the scope of the search warrant. They had my brother Mac and Todd lying on the living room floor. My brother Mac was shocked, because his leg was in a cast from being shot. They had nothing, so they offered Todd time served; but he didn't take the offer 'cause he was still on probation in New York and he would have had to go back to New York. He didn't want to go back 'cause he new I wasn't going back there either. He took three years, and on top of all that, the wrong boy got shot. Luke was supposed to help me out, but, of course, he changed his number and made sure I couldn't get in touch with him. Off to jail Todd went.

Part 6

A NEW LOVE

Todd was in jail, and I divorced him. I started thinking about all the things he did to me and the hell I went through, so I thought to myself, *The perfect revenge*. I started seeing this guy named Steve from Havana, Florida. I met him through my ex-best friend. She was dating his cousin, Mike. My ex-best friend, Mike, Steve, and I went to Pizza Hut for lunch, and that's when we met. I used to go to Havana, where he lived, and he would come to my spot in Tallahassee. We were the perfect couple, so I thought. We used to break up and make up a lot. I remember one time, we broke up, because he thought I was messing around with my brother Marcus's friend Ray. Nothing was going on with us. He was like a brother to me. Real close to the family. Marcus, my oldest sister Tangie, my brother Marcus's baby's mother, and I went to Atlanta to pick up my youngest daughter, Kelly. Me and Steve had an argument before I left. I was calling the house, but Steve was gone. So I called his mother's house in Havana, and Steve was there. He had already packed his clothes and was leaving, but he left his clothes in my house. When I got back, I dropped my sister off and my brother's baby's mother off, then I went to my house. Steve had made it back to my house, and he had his mother's truck there. I had already told Ray he could stay with me, so as Ray was moving in, Steve was moving out—mad as hell. Then we broke up. Steve went back to Tampa with his mother. He stayed there for about three weeks, and we decided to get back together, but I told him there had to be some changes. Steve used to have sex with me once a week, and I wasn't having that. He said because of the situation that I was in, he didn't want to fall in love with me, but it was too late, so he thought that if he left, he would get over me and he would be fine. Steve just couldn't get enough of Free. When he did come back, we were having sex every day. I guess I can say I turned him out. Steve and I got real close, but at one point my ex-best friend and Mike had broken up, and me and Steve were still kicking it. Me and my ex-best friend were so tight that during the summer, we would switch up. She would stay at my house with her three kids at the time and my three kids. It was six children and two adults in a three-bedroom, one-bath house. Then the next summer, we would switch and go to her house, except she lived in a three-bed, two-bath trailer. We were closer than close. I mean my ex-best friend was the first person who introduced me to weed. I smoked my first blunt at the age of twenty-five. I was paranoid as hell. She was like the big sister I never had, but she had mood swings like crazy. When we were fighting, I was toe-to-toe with her, by her side. No one would mess with her unless they messed with me, and most females didn't want to get it. When we would got jumped, I would shielded her from getting hurt. I would take all of her licks. That's how tight we were. We drove each other's cars; fighting was my thang back then. It would be 2:00 a.m., and we would be in the back of the projects parking lot, fighting. My ex-best friend was scary, so I took up the slack for her. Now it was time for the kids to stay at my house. I stopped selling and smoking weed; I had an okay job. I worked, cooked, cleaned, and took care of all the kids while my ex-best friend and Steve were out making so-called money. All they did was ride around, getting high, trying to sell. One day, they got mad at each other—for whatever reason, I don't know. All I know was they were mad at each other. My ex-best friend called me one day to have a conversation with me, and she said that Steve tried her. I was like, "What? How?" She went to explain how he was acting and some things he said to her. The next day, I didn't say anything for a while to Steve. I said I talked to my ex-best friend. He said, "Since we're on the subject about her, I need to watch her." I said, "You can save it, she had already told me." Steve was like, "Baby, guess what, she tried to talk to me." I asked, "Why ya'll both wait until one gets mad at the other to tell everything? I'm in shock here." I got my best friend at the time versus my boyfriend. What do I do? I wanted to hurt both of them real decent. After that, I really stopped talking to both of them. Steve and I are doing good things, making it; but he had a habit I didn't know about. He did it every now and then. I didn't know, because when it came time to pay the bills, he did. He kept a job and was never late. When he messed up, he would do crazy things like drink bleach, etc. All because he didn't want me to be mad at him. I was like, *That's crazy.* Then he would admit himself into the hospital. He did that one too many times, because they Baker Acted his ass the third time. They admitted him to the crazy house for about one week. He didn't do that no more. Steve and my brother Marcus were the best of friends. When you saw one, you saw the other; or you would see all three of us. They were that close. My brother Marcus took Steve with him to rob somebody that owed my brother Marcus some money. Steve had never done that, so he was like, "What the hell," at first, then he was like, "Yeah, we did that shit." It was like a rush for Steve.

Is He Worth It?

One day, Steve decided he would go out after work. It was payday, and I was like, "Okay, cool have fun. I'll be here when you come home." He went to Havana and met up with some old friends, and they started treating their noses; and he had treated his self until he was broke. He realized he hadn't paid any bills, so what he did, he went to this house and rang the doorbell and a lady answered it. He asked if she could help him; it was late, and he had a flat tire and could she help him. The lady was like, "Okay, I'll be right there." (Steve didn't know she was a state trooper.) She had gotten her gun and her car keys to get the jack out of the trunk of her car. The lady went to the truck of her car, opened it, and Steve tried to rob the lady with a fork. She pulled her gun, and they struggled for a minute. Then he bit her, grabbed her gun, took off, and came home as if nothing had happen. Like the time he did this before this last incident—he hit this old man in the stomach, took his wallet, then ran. The cops were after him. He came home flying up the driveway and into the garage. He pushed everything to the back of the garage with the car, then closed the garage. Anyways, the next day, Marcus came to the house. We were reading the paper. I asked Steve what happened to him the night before, and he said, "Don't worry. I got your money." So I wondered where the hell that came from. I started back-reading the paper. I'm in the local part of the paper, and I see a picture that looks just like Steve. I called my brother to the room and told him to look at the picture—it looked just like Steve. My brother was like, "He do, Tasha," then we started reading what happened. Marcus was like, "I knew I should have never taken Steve to rob anyone." (This is just a thought.) See, Marcus only robbed drug dealers, but he always left them with something. Steve was robbing innocent people and so forth. We showed the picture to Steve, and he denied it. Steve said it wasn't him. I was still mad at him. About three days later, I came home from work, and I saw that my house was surrounded by the police. Steve was sitting on the porch, handcuffed; and my kids were inside the house, crying. I asked what was going on. Steve had cooked a lovely meal for us; he was making up with me because we were mad at each other. The officer said, "It's nothing, he'll be out before you know it." I asked him, "What did you do?" Steve said they had a warrant for him for biting his boss. I gave him a kiss and said, "Baby, you'll be out before you know it." I went to see him that night. That's when he told me what he had done. I was like, "Boy, are you crazy? What in the hell were you thinking?" I went and paid for him a lawyer; the best they could do was ten years. It's a damn shame, because he is not a bad person and his record was not long at all. I guess it's just one of those things.

Part 7

MS. THANG

Chapter 3

Oh shit! Where do I begin with this one? It all started in 1998, when Todd got out of jail from shooting that boy in Frenchtown. Todd was in work-release camp, because it was closer time for him to get out. We were divorced, and he wanted to get back with me. Steve had just left to go to prison. Todd was seeing someone else—whom he thought was Tanisha Rollins. Todd and Tanisha had been writing each other, sending pictures; and Tanisha had brought Todd some clothes and money to the work-release place. At the same time, he was trying to get back with me. Todd used to give me money all the time. I was like, "Where are you getting this money from?" He never told me he used to use some guy's car to come and see me. Todd got out and came to see me and the kids. We had sex, and I eventually let him come and live with me. All of a sudden, I'm getting threatening phone calls at work and at home, telling me that they were going to fuck me up! I'm like, "What the hell! Who is this?" My phone was ringing like fifty to sixty times a day. Ms. Thang tells me, "it's" in love with Todd and wants him back. I asked Todd about it, and he didn't know Ms. Thang—not knowing that it was Tanisha Rollins. I had never seen Ms. Thang face to face. I didn't know who that person was on the other end. A couple of weeks went by, and Todd was in the projects, shooting the shit with the boys; and the project was thick. This car pulled up, and it looked as though two females are in there. The girl on the passenger side got out, and Todd saw her. Todd was looking at the girl like, *I know you.* It was the picture that was sent to him; it was Tanisha Rollins. Todd said to the girl, "What's up?" The girl spoke, then went apologizing to Todd. She said she didn't know that it would go this far. Todd had this puzzled look on his face. Ms. Thang got all of his information from when she was a correctional officer at the facility that Todd was at. Ms. Thang was fired for messing with inmates and bringing in drugs. Ms. Thang knew all of my personnel information, and that *bitch* used it to her advantage. Ms. Thang also went to jail for making phony credit cards; she went to law school at FSU. "Its" father died and left it a whole lot of money (so they say). This is just a little background of the psycho. The girl started crying, then Ms. Thang got out of the car and said, "I'm Tanisha Rollins." Ms. Thang is a MAN! Oh my God! Before you knew it, Todd had knocked Ms. Thang to the ground. Ms. Thang got up hollering, crying, and grabbing its mouth, bleeding. Ms. Thang did that in front of all the boys, and then threw some letters Todd had written to Tanisha Rollins. You know Todd wasn't going to let that slide. Ms. Thang got up, ran into the car, and started it up; and Ms. Thang had its window down and was backing out when Todd was hopping on one foot and stomping Ms. Thang with the other foot. Steve had on Timberlands too, and he knocked out three of Ms. Thang's teeth. Ms. Thang had to get stitches. Todd went back to jail. While he was in there, Todd found a way to get in touch with Ms. Thang and talked Ms. Thang into dropping the charges. Ms. Thang went to the prosecutor's office, telling them he didn't want to press charges. Ms. Thang started yelling when they told it that the state was going to pick up the charges. Ms. Thang acted like a donkey.

At the same time, Todd started talking to some girl from Monticello, Florida. They were talking, and I again broke it off with Todd, because I was like, "This is too much for me." Todd called with his new girlfriend on the phone. He wanted to talk to the kids. I let him, and then he asked me to talk to his new friend about Ms. Thang. I briefly explained to her what it was like. I don't know how, when, or what, but Todd and his new friend and Ms. Thang called me fussing about who was going to be with Todd. So was like, "What the hell are you all calling me for?" Everybody was fussing, and Todd kept telling Ms. Thang to please leave him alone—he was not gay and would never be gay. He loved pussy all day. How can a gay person only go out with someone who is not gay? Hello, like I said earlier—PSYCHO! Everybody was still fussing, and his new friend got beside herself. I knew when she said what she said, I should have let it go, but I didn't. Todd's new friend said, "I don't care what anybody says"—Ms. Thang had been blowing her phone up—"Todd is coming home to me, and there's nothing anyone can do about it." I said to myself, *It's on.* Todd called me the day he was getting out, asking for me to take him back. I said, "Okay, I'll pick you up from the jail tonight." It was twelve midnight; Todd was getting out, and I was picking him up. We got home and had sex (first round). My phone wa ringing. It was his new friend asking if I hadheard from Todd, and I told her, "He's right here." She started crying and asked me why I did that to her. I told her, "Never underestimate me. I can get him anytime I want, and you tried me." Then I gave Todd the phone. He told her, "I told you if my ex-wife takes me back, I would go back to her." They talked for about five minutes and hung up. Then the phone rang again, and we ignored it. Todd and I started having sex again, and the phone kept ringing. And it was Ms. Thang. I put the phone on the dresser with the mouthpiece facing up, and I started moaning saying, "Ooh, Todd, right there. Ooh that feels so damn good." I picked up the phone, and Ms. Thang was crying like a little bitch. After that, it was on. Now the stalking started.

Part 8

THE STALKING BEGINS

Part 2

Ms. Thang stalked me from 1999 to 2001. So for two years, I was stalked and harassed. Ms. Thang made my life a living hell. I felt as if I was making a movie. It was so unreal. Ms. Thang said he was going to stalk me until I killed myself. He said he had stalked someone like that before, and they finally killed themselves. I told Ms. Thang that would never happen, because I loved myself too much. It was about 7:00 p.m. now, and I still didn't know what Ms. Thang looked like. Someone was yelling, blowing their horn, getting out of the car, and yelling up and down my street. Neighbors were looking. I called the sheriff's department (on top of that, I'm living about six houses down from my mother's house), and an officer came out and asked what was going on, and I told him, "I don't know who that person is, but it looks like a man dressed up as a woman." The officer asked why that person was out there disturbing the peace. I didn't know why, because I had never met Ms. Thang. I didn't know that was the person making my life a living hell. I went outside to get a better look, and Ms. Thang had blue contacts in his eyes, a blonde bob wig, and a miniskirt on. All I could think of it, *What the fuck! Is this a joke?* He was like, "I can't stand that bitch!" pointing at me. I'm saying to myself *Ms. Thang's got a dick. Ms. Thang is stalking me, because he wants my husband.* Todd was like, "What do you want from me?" Ms. Thang said, "I want that Tommy bath robe, Tommy slippers, and Tommy PJ set." And Todd was like, "How you know about that?" Ms. Thang said, "I bought all of that shit!" Todd gave it to the officer to give it to Ms. Thang. Then Todd told the officer to tell Ms. Thang not to bother us again. The officer was like, "Who is that female?" Todd said, "That is a man." The officer opened the door, looked outside, then closed the door, looked at me and Todd, and said, "Are you serious?" We were like, "Yeah." The officer had a look like I never saw. I wanted to laugh so bad, but it was a serious matter, so the officer told Ms. Thang. Now, I was looking at this motherfucker like something just wasn't cutting it right about now. I had never heard anything about Todd turning gay while he was in jail. You know the streets talk. We lay down, he went right to sleep, and I'm up thinking. Ms. Thang called so much, I took the phone off the hook. Then the next day, Ms. Thang went and called my case worker at HRS, telling her all kinds of shit that wasn't true—telling them I had stocks and bonds, land, and a house I was renting out. All that stuff wasn't true, but of course, they had to investigate it. After about two weeks, they saw it was lie; then he kept calling and kept calling Todd's probation officer, trying to get Todd violated. He told Todd's PO that Todd and I tried to run him and his grandmother over. Then he paid someone to break into my phone box on the side of my house, and they would call his phone. Then he would take the phone to Todd's PO and say that Todd called him. We had called the sheriff's department and told them what Ms. Thang was doing, and one officer came out and was so unprofessional. We told the officer about the box on the side of the house; he didn't believe us. I told him he could keep his personal opinion to his self and to just do his job then leave. He went to take fingerprints but didn't use any gloves. When I called his supervisor and told him how he was acting the things he said and that he didn't use gloves to do fingerprints, the supervisor apologized and sent out another officer. The second officer was so nice and kind, but he mainly got the first officer's prints. Anyways, Todd's PO asked us if we could move out of town. I said, "Why should we have to move? Why can't y'all tell Ms. Thang to stop calling?" I said no one was going to make me leave, and I stayed. The next thing I know I'm getting service papers for a protection injunction in Gadsden County (Quincy, Florida). Todd and I went to court, but Ms. Thang didn't show up. About one month later, I get service papers again for Leon County (Tallahassee, Florida). He didn't show up again. Then Todd's PO called again, saying Ms. Thang said Todd just tried to kill him, but Todd was at work when it supposedly happened. Then one day, Todd started working out of town, and then my kids came home from school, and I was still at work. My children had a routine—when they came home from school, they changed clothes, got them a snack, got their homework tighter, then walked up to my mom's house until I got home. It was a Thursday, and my kids were at my parents' house. I came home to find out Ms. Thang had went to my parents house dressed up in a police officer's uniform, asking questions about me and Todd. Ms. Thang had spoken with my oldest daughter. She didn't know at the time who Ms. Thang was, but when Ms. Thang started to be rude, my daughter went in the house and got my mother. My mother thought it was a real police officer and gave Ms. Thang a little information about me. So when I came home, my daughter went to tell me a police officer was looking for me. I asked, "Did he leave a card?" She told me she didn't know and to ask my mother because the officer had talked with my mother. I asked my mom. She said, "No he didn't," so I called the police station, and no one went to my mother's house; and they said they didn't need to talk to me. I thought it was odd, because the police didn't go to my parents' house. Where they live—it's the sheriff's jurisdiction, not the police. I called the sheriff's office and let them know what he did. It was so hard trying to stay focused when someone has all of your personal information and could mess your whole life up. Ms. Thang had every type of information that a criminal would want. Ms. Thang would call my parents' house and hold a conversation with my mother about me and Todd. Ms. Thang pretended to be a friend of Todd and would tell my mother all kinds of lies about Todd, and my mother would believe it, because she didn't like Todd. Any dirt anyone tells my mom about Todd, she would believe it. I didn't blame my mother, but sometimes you need to let your child find out the hard way, because when it comes to love, you could be so blind to it, but a blind man could see it. I know my mother meant no harm to me, and she only wanted the best for me; but Mom needed to let me handle it and at least be on my side. Ms. Thang had my parents' social security numbers and their banking account information. That's why I was so afraid, not because of the stalking, but because this psycho had all of my information in his possession, and there wasn't anything I could do about it. I couldn't prove it, and it is so hard to build a stalking case, because of the way the law is. How many times have you heard of a spouse who gets out of an abusive relationship and gets a restraining order, then turns around and gets killed? The laws on stalking need to be revised and taken more seriously. Ms. Thang must have been watching me and my kids' routine, because on the day my kids came home, changed clothes, and before they could go to my mom's house, there was a knock at the door. The door was locked. My oldest daughter looked out the window and saw a small black car in the driveway. Then she looked toward the door, and a man was standing there with a gun. The man kept knocking, and my daughter called the sheriff's department; and they came to the house, and my daughter told them what happened. So they stayed there until I got home. The officer said they didn't have much to go on, and advised me to go to see Victim's Advocate and seek help. Then the officer told me to be careful, because this stalker knew the law—and that was why he hadn't been caught. Todd came back and reported to his PO. They said this stalker was getting on their nerves and that they are tired of him, so I went and filed a restraining order against him. I had a case with victim advocate. We went to court, and Ms. Thang showed up; and we went before a judge. Ms. Thang was so rude to the judge. Ms. Thang kept trying to cut me off when I was explaining to the judge all the things he was doing to me and my family. The judge kicked him out, because the judge kept asking Ms. Thang to keep quiet and to control his self. He acted as though he didn't hear a word the judge was trying to say, so the judge kicked him out and granted me my judgment. I was working at the *Tallahassee Democrat* newspaper when Ms. Thang kept calling me. He would harass me at work so many times till it didn't make any sense. The night of the day we went to court, Ms. Thang kept calling me; he went to the sheriff's office, raising all kinds of hell, lying, and saying I was harassing him. They put a warrant out on me. Ms. Thang told the sheriff's office he had a restraining order out on me and showed them the papers he filed in Quincy, Florida. I called the sheriff's office the next day, in the afternoon, to let them know that Ms. Thang was still stalking me (three years had passed now). So the officer on duty told me there was a warrant out for me for violating a restraining order. I explained to the officer that Ms. Thang didn't have a restraining order against me, that he never showed up for court, and that the judge ruled in my favor. I told the officer I had one against him and that mine was legal. The officer told me, "Here's what I'll do, because we are so tired of this man." He told me to be careful going home, he was going to do away with the warrant, but it was going to take a day. He said that if I get pulled over, they were going to have to arrest me until they could clear this mess up. I did just that. I went home and waited until the next day. Ms. Thang was calling like crazy still. After about three more days, I had enough. On the third day, I went to see Victim's Advocate and told them I was about to lose my mind. Ms. Thang would not leave me alone, and it was as if we were playing tit for tat with the sheriff's department. They were tired of me and him, but what was I supposed to do? They told me to keep a log of everything that was going on—like dates, time, and what Ms. Thang said or did. I did just that. On the night of the third day, the phone calls began. After the twentieth phone call, I finally was able to get through to the sheriff's office, and I requested an officer to come to the house and do a report. They sent one out, but in the meantime, they were telling me what I could do to trace the calls—and I did. When the officer arrived, my phone was ringing off the hook. The officer called the station back and told another officer, "We need to do something about this right away, because I've been here for twenty minutes, and this phone hasn't stopped ringing." The officer said he could only imagine what I'd been going through. They traced the call to a phone booth by his house, where they arrested him on the spot for stalking. The next day, I went to his bond hearing along with some detectives who had been helping me with my cases as well as my case worker from victim advocate. They spoke on my behalf, and he got a bond for fifty thousand dollars, but no bond on his probation violation (I didn't know that all that time, he was on probation in Jefferson county for making false credit cards). He hired a lawyer, and I took it to trial. I had the sheriff's officer who was there to witness the harassment as my witness. I testified, and Ms. Thang's lawyer turned it all around. He said the sheriff's office mistreated him because he was gay. As I was on the stand, I kept noticing one white male juror looking at Ms. Thang. Then every now and then, he would shake his head up and down. After all that, they found Ms. Thang not guilty. Talk about your jurors. I believe he paid that man off. My case was strong and solid. After he was released, it got even crazier. He really started stalking me, except he was more careful. I had to have an escort from the campus police to and from my classes at the college (Tallahassee Community College). My professor was concerned with me 'cause I had stopped coming, and my work wasn't as good as it was; and when the day came, I went back to class and my professor had talked to me in her office and she asked what was going on with me. My professor was a lawyer. I explained it to her; she was so shocked. And she was like, "This sounds like a movie. Oh my God. I can't believe what you're going through." She worked with me and also told me I needed to do a book about this. After about one month, I said, "The hell with this, let's move out of town." Todd's PO was too happy, he was like, "Now maybe he could get some peace of mind." We moved to Port St. Joe, Florida, found an apartment, and moved in. Now after all of that, Todd took me through so much shit again.

Part 9

ENOUGH IS ENOUGH

Ms. Thang was still bothering us, but it was not as bad, because we didn't have a house phone. Todd got a good job in Panama City, Florida, and he carpooled with some of the neighbors who work with him. He went out in Panama City and met some new people, and he was back into the street life. Everything was good for about four months. Instead of him being a man saying "Let's move to Panama City 'cause there's a lot of opportunity for us there," he started cheating again. We were having fights; then one day, I said I was going to try and make this relationship work (remember, we were not married anymore). I wasn't working, he was; and I had a claim going on with Worker's Comp. I had hurt my back on the job. I always had him a hot meal when he came home, the house was always clean, and I had his stuff ready for a shower when he got home. This particular day, everything was the same. He came home to a hot meal, clean house, and stuff ready for a shower. We ate and watched TV; it was around 7:00 p.m. when he jumped in the shower. I had the bedroom set up perfect. I had the candles lit, petals on the bed, and the slow music going. When he got out the shower, he was shocked. We had freaky, nasty, good sex for about one and a half hours. Around 9:00 p.m., Todd said his head was hurting and he was going to the store to get something for his headache. I said okay. Eleven o'clock passed—no Todd. I thought, *Well, maybe he saw somebody and was shooting the breeze with them.* Half past midnight—no Todd, but I heard a knock on my door. It was Amy (my brother Mac's baby's mama). She said she saw my car at the store parking lot and that the lady at the store said she saw Todd get in the car with this girl named Shawn. My youngest daughter, Kelly, and I got dressed. I knew I should not have woken her up, but I was pissed. We got dressed, and I got my gun. I told Amy to take me to get my car. She did. I went and parked my car behind the apartment complex so I could see the bridge from there. I was outside sitting on the trunk of my car, talking to Amy and her sister about Todd. My daughter Kelly was in the backseat of the car, playing. Two in the morning came around, and I saw her car coming over the bridges. So

I jumped in my car, and when I got to the stop sign, I waited till she passed, then followed her. I stayed a distance until I saw her pull up at the store where my car was. When she went to park, I pulled in real fast behind her, then Todd jumped out of her car. I went to the driver side and was trying to get her to let her window down, but that trick wouldn't work. She kept saying nothing happened. My thing was, "You knew we were together, so what the *fuck* are you doing riding around with him?" Todd kept saying, "Tasha, stop, let me explain. Nothing happened." Before I knew it, I went back to my car, because I couldn't believe this asshole was trying to talk to me. I got my gun (the one I bought when Ms. Thang started bothering me) and pointed it at him. Took it off safe, and I was trying to pull the trigger, at the same time trying to pull the clip back. It was a .45 automatic; I couldn't cock the gun back in time. You should have seen him running and hollering. Everyone was yelling. Shawn drove her car up on the sidewalk of the store, hitting shit, trying to get the hell out or dodge. After that, Todd came home, packed his stuff, and left. One week had passed since the gun incident, and I hadn't been out in a long time, so I went and got my hair done; and at the place were I was getting my car done, the girl—Shawn—was there. So the guy who was doing my hair pulled me outside and said, "Tasha, Shawn is a little nervous, and she wants to talk to you about that night. Will you talk to her without hitting or shooting?" I told him sure. Shawn and I went outside and talked. She said nothing happened between her and Todd, but he came to her in the store and said he wanted to talk, so he got in her car and they went to Panama City and talked. I told her, "That's all fine, but you knew he was married, and you should have told him to 'go home and talk to your wife' and left, but it's all good." I told her, "There are no hard feelings, I'm over it. Hell, he isn't even worth it." I got dressed up, and I rode with Shawn to the club, and who do I see? Mr. Todd. He saw me and his mouth just dropped. I was looking so damn good, he didn't know what to do; and then I found out he was staying with some girl who was a correctional officer. She was at the club. He had no choice but to introduce us, because she was on his dick. Todd kept following me around, telling me I better not talk to anyone. I told him to kiss the crack of my ass and move the hell on. I got so many numbers that night, and I had a good time watching Todd get mad at the guys who were getting all of my attention while he wasn't getting any. Then he had the nerve to approach one guy and tell him that I was his wife and that he needed to talk to me. The guy looked at me. I told Todd there was nothing to talk about. "You are here with your new girl, so go head on." The guy and I got on the dance floor and had a good time. After the club closed, Todd asked me to go with him and get a room together. I told him, "Why pay for a room when I got my own place I can go to for free?" I told Todd I was going to bring him Kelly the next day and not to make any plans. As time went by, I was behind on bills and Todd wasn't giving me any money to help out—so I joined the army.

Part 10

JOINING THE MILITARY

Chapter 4

After all the bullshit, I still loved him. I wasn't working, and I had the kids—he knew that. He was the biggest whore in Panama City. New booty. Oh yeah, he was the shit. Quit his job to hang out in the streets. A month passed, and I still wasn't working; but I was going to school and my lights were about to get cut off. I called Todd, and he told me that he was going to help—but that was a lie. I went to Panama City to get the money, and he introduced me to this fat girl he was staying with. I was like, "Whatever." A couple of days went by, and he gave me $100. I was like, "A hundred dollars, are you serious?" Then he told me he was tired of the streets and that he wanted to come home. I was like, "Okay 'cause I really needed the help." Then he met this other girl whom I found out he had a key to the house to and that he'd moved in with her. The whole time, he was lying to me. Something happened there, and his PO came by the house looking for him. Of course, I covered for him. I told him I needed his help. "I'm in school, and Kelly is not in day care. Could you come home?" He said he wanted to come back with me and that we would talk about it (this bitch is the one who did me wrong and I'm begging him back). We went back to Port St. Joe and talked. He told me that if I let him have anal sex with me, he'd come back home. I just started crying, because I couldn't believe he would say that to me. He knew I wasn't working, and that I depended on him for the first time, and he pulled this shit. My feelings were so hurt; I thought I was better than that to him. So I said okay. As we tried it, it hurt real bad, then I told him to stop and not go in any further, to take it out. He kept saying, "I only put the head in." I told him, "I don't care. Take it out. It hurts too bad." Tears were rolling down my face, and all he said was, "You have to relax your muscles," and then starts kissing me in the back of my neck. I told him, "No! *Fuck* this, it hurts too bad," then he told me to take him back to Panama City, and he didn't even help me. After a few days of crying, I woke up one morning, got on my knees, and prayed—then told myself, *FUCK that NIGGA! I've always been strong and independent. I can make it.* I did something I'd always wanted to do—and that was join the army. Here went Ms. Thang, calling my case, working in

Port St. Joe, telling them I had land in my name. They started doing their investigation. After I joined, I didn't have to leave until January, because I was still in college. I was behind on my rent, so when I moved in December, I sold all of my furniture and it went to my landlord. One day, I went outside and I saw white stuff by my gas tank—it was sugar. I asked my neighbor if they saw anyone by my car, and they described to me Ms. Thang's car. I went to the police department and made a report. It was a very small town, so they didn't even know were to begin to help me, because he was from Tallahassee. After I completely moved out, I called my landlord to make sure I didn't owe any money, and they said I was good. Three days later, my landlord called me and told me that this guy called them, inquiring about getting an apartment, but he wanted the one I was staying in. Ms. Thang met with my landlord and started asking them questions about me, asking if they knew where I was and where I worked. My landlord cut the conversation off and told Ms. Thang they would get back in touch with him. Then they called me and told me what was going on. I couldn't believe Ms. Thang was following me. I called Tallahassee, and there was nothing they could do because it was out of their jurisdiction. I moved to Panama City and stayed with a friend until it was time for me to go to basic training. The kids were in Tallahassee with my parents. I let my case worker know as well as the FBI, because of the welfare fraud investigation. I was still messing with Todd on the sly, and three days before I left, Todd took me out to eat at Applebee's. He got a phone call and told me he needed to make a sting real quick and that he would be right back. I was getting drunk as hell, and he came back about thirty minutes later. I was pissed and drunk; I couldn't leave because he used my car. He brought me a teddy bear with candy. I looked at him like whatever. So we ate, and then we got into an argument about something, so we left Applebee's fussing. I was driving and he hit me, so I let the steering wheel go and went at it with him (I was drunk as hell). He grabbed the steering wheel and then we pulled over to a gas station down the street from where he was staying. He asked me to take him to the strip club, I said okay. I took him there. Whoever he was looking for wasn't there, so he came out. We were still fussing, he told the officer at the door that we were arguing and that I had a gun, so if anything happen to him, I did it. The officer just laughed. We were going back to his spot, we got into it again. He got out and started walking, so I went to his spot and waited for him. He lost his keys in my car, and we were looking for them. A car pulled up, and it was a girl name Trina. She spoke, I spoke, and then she asked Todd what was up. He said, "Nothing, just looking for my keys." Then she said, "Well, baby, were did you last seen them?" Before he could answer, I said, "Baby." She was like, "Yeah," so I asked her, "Who are you?" She said, "Trina, T-Lo's girlfriend." I was like, "OOH HELL NAW!" She asked me who I was, I told her, "His wife." We both were going off on Todd. I got in my car, then he got in the passenger side (I didn't ask him to). We're riding, and she's following us. I told him, "If she hits my car, it's on." I was still going off on him. She was calling his cell, telling him he better give her the keys to her house, the money she gave him, and the stuff she bought him. I finally said, "Fuck this shit," and pulled over. As I went to get out of the car, Todd told me to stay in the car and that he would handle it. He threw her the keys to her house, snatched the necklace off his neck, and threw it to her. Told Trina not to come around him and not to call him (all game). She was like, "Cool. Don't freaking call me either." I was on my way back to my friend's house, where I was staying. He was in the car with me. We were talking, and he went to use the bathroom; and he was on the phone with Trina, making up a lie to get back with her. Todd knew I was on my way to basic training. I told him it was over—and fuck him. When I dropped him off, he said something to piss me off, so I tried to hit him with my car. I mean, I went up on the porch steps trying to run is ass over. Off to basic training I went.

Part 11

FBI IS LOOKING FOR ME

I was at basic training in Fort Jackson, South Carolina; it was the year 2000. I was there for about four months, and my first sergeant sent for me. Todd had told my unit I was not taking care of home. Now first of all, for some reason, I was not getting paid, and another thing—we were not together anymore, and he didn't have the kids. They made me send money home to him. While all of this was going on, Ms. Thang was causing more problems. He heard I went to the army. He went to the Panama City Recruiting Station, asking questions about me. Then he called the FBI, causing big problems. Instead of doing more investigation and waiting until I finished basic training and AIT (Advance Individual Training), they issued a warrant for my arrest. I was at the end of basic training when my drill sergeant called for me and two other soldiers to ride with her. Drill sergeant talked to everyone in the van but me. We got to the barracks; she opened up a door with all of our personal stuff, and told me to get my bag and put on civilian clothes. I was shocked, and I started crying because I was thinking they were putting me out because I had bought some candy when I wasn't supposed to and I was selling it. I changed into civilian clothes and got in the van. Drill sergeant still wasn't saying anything to me, so I asked her where we were going. She said, "To jail." I yelled "JAIL! I didn't do anything, I'm sorry about the candy, Drill Sergeant." She said, "It's not the army." I got there crying my eyes out, and they said I had a warrant in Tallahassee, Florida. I asked, "For what?" They said, "For welfare fraud." I stopped crying 'cause I knew who was behind it. I asked if I could use the phone, and I called my mom to tell her what was going on. She just laughed. I told her I was serious. I asked her to take the block off the phone so I could call, but she wouldn't. She said it cost too much ($15). I got to the jail, and I was calling like crazy. I called home, and my brother Marcus was like, "Sis, don't cry, you better not cry." So I stopped crying and changed my whole look. He said, "I'm going to see what I can do." Then I called Mr. Todd and told him I was in jail. He went off; he was mad as hell. He was like, "That punk motherfucker." I told him, "You better get me out of here. It's your fault that I'm in here!" He tried, but I had no bond in South Carolina I had a bond in Tallahassee. I just had to get there. They put me in this holding cell for about four hours; it was cold as hell in there. I thought I was going to lose my mind. Finally, they fingerprinted me, then I had to undress in front of the guard. I didn't care 'cause, hell, I had to take a shower with about sixty other females. I changed into my orange jailhouse outfit, and they took me to the back. I walked in, looking like, *This can't be happening to me, this is just a dream.* Everyone was looking at the new booty coming in. I didn't say anything; they showed me where I was sleeping. I had to sleep on a mattress on the floor, next to the toilet. My cellmate was cool. When she got her commissary, she shared it with me. I had money, but no way of getting it. My hair was braided to the back, so of course I looked like a dyke. The next day, they let us go outside in the yard (a very, very small one), doing push-ups and exercising. There was a basketball court, but no ball. So this one girl kept looking at me—I spoke, she spoke—I kept on exercising. This girl thought I was a dyke and came on to me. I had to tell her, "I have three children. I love dick all day and all night. I like to suck it and fuck it." So her "boyfriend" got upset and approached me. She said, "What's up?" I said, "What's up?" Then she asked me if I liked her girl. Everything my brother Marcus told me was going through my head. He told me people who have been in jail before can tell when you haven't, and they prey on that. He told me to always stand my ground. That's what I did. I told her I'm not a dyke and that I have a boyfriend. She wasn't trying to hear that. She kept talking about what she would do to me. I told her to do it. "If you think you can handle me, then go for it." She started talking some more and slowly started walking toward me. So I walked faster to her and got in her face, and I told her, "Fuck all that talk, do something." She backed up, shaking her head up and down. I told her, "What you want to do?" She didn't say anything else. After that, we were cool. One day, we were out of our cells for dinner and this inmate asked me if I wanted my corn bread. I told her yeah; she said she should take it. I told her, "Try it," then we both stood up and started toward each other. The CO broke us up and told me if I got into any more trouble, they would send me to Zulo land. That was the jail hole box. It was nothing in there—just plain white walls, a sink, and a toilet. No mattress or anything else. You stay in there twenty-three hours and thirty minutes. The other thirty minutes was for you to take a shower. We were only allowed out of our rooms for two hours a day. In the morning, we took a shower two at a time. There were only two showers. I had to wash my underwear out with the soap they provided for me, and I wore them wet, because I had no one to buy me any. So I had kept a rash for your ass from wearing wet draws.

You were usually allowed out of the room two hours in the morning or two hours in the evening. The only person who would accept my calls was my auntie Felicia. She would call my daddy's house on three—way for me. If I was out in the morning, I wasn't able to call, because my auntie would be at work. I called every other day. A month had passed, and it started getting to me. I would bang my head against the door. I thought I was going to lose my mind. My cellmate started praying and talking to me to calm me down. I finally was able to see the judge. Now I had never seen anything like this before. They took me to his office, which looked like a run-down house. He didn't have a robe on or anything to the nature of a judge. He had a perm, like Al Sharpener. Hell, I thought he was Al Sharpener. Anyways, it took about two months to get me to Tallahassee. I even heard my unit graduated from basic training. Talk about being heartbroken; I was so hurt. I went to jail two weeks before graduation from basic training. Ain't that a bitch!

Part 12

BACK TO "T" TOWN

I was in Tallahassee, holding cell. All I needed was $50 to get out, and do you know my mother didn't want to pay it? My daddy came through for me. I love my daddy. When I finally got released, my daddy was the first person I saw. I went and took care of some things and, of course, called Todd. I spent time with my kids, and Todd came and got me. We went back to Panama City; he had his own place, and we had sex. Then at first, he didn't want me to move in with him. So I told him to get Kelly, because I couldn't afford day care, and my mom and I were bumping heads. I was tired, so Todd was like, "Come on." Kelly and I moved to Panama City, Florida, again. My other two children stayed with my mom until we could get a bigger place. After moving, about three months later, Todd and I went out, and when we came home, there was a message on the phone saying Todd needed to call his uncle. When he called, Todd got the news that his brother had just died. He was hit by a car, and then three other cars ran over him. They found four different track marks on his body. His body was decapitated from the waist, and it was mangled. The front of his chest was caved all the way to his back. What a horrible death! We went to Fort Walton Beach to tell his stepdad (who was white, but cool as hell). I remember when we went to the beach and tried to have sex in the water, but it didn't work. It hurt to bad. We went to the funeral—it was so sad. Everyone thought his mother was going to be able to come from prison, but I guess the prison she was at wouldn't let her come. I know Todd's stepfather was looking forward to seeing her, but I don't know about his real father. His mother was in prison for trying to set her house on fire with her husband and kids inside. His mother had flipped out. He was only twenty-seven years old when he died, and he was about ten feet from his grandmother's house. He was going home when he was hit by a car, and the driver was some young boy who went all the way home and got his parents—and he told the cops he thought he hit a deer. The boy who hit him and left only got three years probation, and then the cops said that Todd's brother was walking on the wrong side of the street—now that's some BS. There were no streetlights on that road, and that road is very dark and dangerous at night. Once again, Ms. Thang tried to find a way to see Todd by lying, saying Todd and I were calling, bothering him. It didn't work; the sheriff's department tried to get Ms. Thang to come down to the station and make a report so they could get him for making a false police report. They were so tired of him. Hell, years had passed by and he was still up to his tricks. He went to the state attorney's office so much, raising all kinds of hell, until they told him that if he came back up there, they were going to arrest him. He would go up there, yelling at them, asking them why they haven't arrested Todd yet. Then about one week later, he would go back up there yelling at them, telling them he wasn't going to press charges against Todd. They asked him why Ms. Thang said he was in love with Todd, so the prosecutor asked Ms. Thang, "Does Todd feel the same way about you?" Ms. Thang said, "Todd isn't gay. I'm gay. I don't do gay men." The prosecutor said, "Something is not right upstairs with that man—lights on, but nobody's home." This went on for months. The prosecutor kept telling him, "We can't arrest someone who doesn't want you. Todd is happily married, and you need to leave him and his family alone before we lock you up again. Now do not come back up here unless you have a legitimate case." Before we left to go back to Panama City, a lot of things were going through my mind. Todd, his brother dying—my mother and I weren't getting along, I decided to take a drive alone. Who do I see at the store? Ms. Thang. I was in a car he never saw before, with tints on the windows. I was in the car, waiting on him to come out, and then I followed him. He mad a couple of stops before going home. I was already dressed in black, and I had my sneakers on. When he got out of his car, I sneaked up behind him, grabbed him by the neck from behind, and slung him to the ground. I started punching him and kicking him in the face. It was like all the rage I ever had just came out. At first, I couldn't control myself, then all of a sudden, I stopped when I saw he wasn't moving—then I took off. I went to my sister's house. I was calm. I acted as if nothing ever happened. They were smoking, and I had started drinking. I was watching the news to see if he reported anything, but he never did. I never saw or heard from him again. (Now that is what I was thinking about doing to him?)

All in all, there were bad times then good times. I've been through a lot and took a lot, and that's what made me stronger. Never let a man disgrace you in any way. Always know that you are better than that and that you're a beautiful person. If he tells you that "no man isn't going to want a woman with kids" (all ready-made family), that's bullshit. He knows he lost you, so he is going to say whatever he has to, to try and keep you. I know parents can be overprotective of their children, and that's understandable; but when it comes to love, the best thing a parent can do is first, try and talk to your child and let them know that what is happening to them is wrong. Love doesn't leave bruises. Love don't call you a whore or a bitch. If your child still doesn't want to listen, then let that child learn on his own. Always be there for your child, be that shoulder they lean on when they need to cry. Don't push them away by saying, "If you're going to be with him, then we don't want anything to do with you," because if he hears that, then it's all games for him. Your child will really be mistreated and your child will feel as if they can't come to you, so they sit there and take it. Always let your child know that they can always come home and you're there if they need you. You may think that your child isn't listening, but they are; then eventually your child will come around and start making the right choices. They will realize that they deserve better and they don't have to put up with the bullshit.

Always be independent, never depend on a man for nothing. That's something my mom always taught me. Whatever choices you make in life, make sure it's what you and no one else wants, or it will not work. Whatever you do make, sure that your home is happy. Take care of your family.

Now is he worth it? Did I give him another chance?